SEASONINGS

Written and Illustrated by Lula Joughin Dovi

Order this book online at www.trafford.com
or email orders@trafford.com

Most Trafford titles are also available at major online book retailers.

Printed in the United States of America.

ISBN: 978-1-4269-6192-2 (sc)
ISBN: 978-1-4269-6193-9 (hc)
ISBN: 978-1-4269-6194-6 (e)

Library of Congress Control Number: 2011904406

Trafford rev. 03/28/2011

 www.trafford.com

North America & international
toll-free: 1 888 232 4444 (USA & Canada)
phone: 250 383 6864 ♦ fax: 812 355 4082

ABOUT THE AUTHOR

A fourth-generation native of Tampa, Lula Joughin Dovi received a B.A. degree from Florida State University and an M.A. degree from University of South Florida. She spent 37 years in the Hillsborough County Public Schools system as teacher and curriculum coordinator. During World War II she was briefly a reporter and editor for Associated Press in San Diego. Now 88, she has been publishing personal recollections and reading her poetry with two different groups. She created the accompanying artwork.

Her children are: son Enrico; daughter Marguerite, married to Kurt Feichtmeir, who have two daughters, Alicia and Nora, and a son Anton; and daughter Lucretia, married to Michael Hilson, who have a daughter Astrid.

ACKNOWLEDGMENT

My gratitude goes to Lucretia Hilson, Jaime Butner and Toni Lupo for their help in the assembling of this publication.

DEDICATION

To my family including my deceased husband, Stefano Dovi, father of our children, Enrico, Marguerite and Lucretia as well as grandfather of our grandchildren, Anton, Alicia, Nora and Astrid;

To poet friends, other friends and teachers;

To the pilgrimage of the human spirit seeking illumination;

I dedicate these verses.

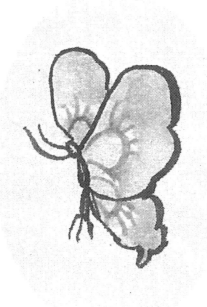

ANOTHER EPOCH

I wrote so proudly about them—
my great grandmother and her mother—
and how they faced their losses
in the Civil War.
But they were slaveholders.

The Union Army torched their home,
a stately home among the
heights of Mt. Airy in Virginia.
They had been slaveholders.

When the home was gone—
after the second Union invasion of their land—
they had to live in the slave quarters
where their slaves had lived.

Leaving their cherished homestead
they escaped to Memphis
but were beset by yellow fever.
The plague took down great grandmother,
her mother and a brother.

What happened to the slaves?

FAMILY SECRETS

Family secrets enclosed inside
  the family circle—
forms of familiarity
only for some—
  interred by death.
From frayed circle
  dead names finally come to me
  from father's secret life.
                    Decades pulled our lives apart.
Half- sister
  known about too late—
  a widowed duchess dead at 40—
  student of Chiapas Indians,
  her legacy in Mexico.
                    My regrets.

DISAPPEARANCES

You never really saw them
 but somehow they were there
 stored in her lively thoughts
 or even stirring up
 the child's delight with
 wonder and caprice
 of coming and going,
 stepping out of storyland
 to star for one long entr'acte—
 until twixt-teen.

No formal farewells, merely fading
 silenced by the closing storybook
 of Santa Clause, Easter Bunny, Leprechaun,
 wizards, witches, fairies and a dragon or two.

THE BULLDOZER CAME

Then it seemed so large, but later so much smaller,
and now it's gone completely.
The two-story Dutch colonial,
a house that hugged us closely in its early years,
fell before the bulldozer,
gasped its last for the sake of suburban condos.

No more sliding down the banister
or sitting on the porch
beneath the giant live-oak.

Fireplace memories, stories told,
our lives twined bright as the coals that warmed us.
Before we left we picked bouquets in each season.

We sang so many songs around the piano
with the violin accompanying.

Then came war, college, marriages, separations and deaths.
Now everyone is gone.
I am the only one that viewed the final passing.

WHEN THE WORLD WAS SMALL

When I was young the world was small.
Time trailed an unmarked ribbon before me
  always blowing, following a wind
  breathing a quicksand moment—
    brief encounter with a doodle bug stirred from his sandy hole—
    listening to the whippoorwill at night—
    watching "bulbats" flit about a power pole—
    studying a big locust, gaudy gold, brown and green—
    catching fireflies for peanut butter jar lanterns—
    keeping polliwogs in a bowl in my bedroom.

Time corkscrewed, the ribbon wrapped,
 little world spun outward into an unknown orbit
  without bats, fireflies, whippoorwill, locust.
  Well-sprayed suburbs grewww…and grewww…and grewww.

SANS SELVAGE

...”Sleep that knits up the ravell'd sleave of care...”
From *Macbeth*, by William Shakespeare

Some dreams close with a selvage finish:
  painful fissures of the psyche
  hemmed together
  with healing stitches,
 or ravelings woven neatly by sleep,
 dread overlaid by comfort.
But mending fails when my father
 enters my dreams with problems unreconciled:
  I forgot to call him so many times;
  that is the fiction of the dream.
His deathbed rejection allows no selvage edge
 in fact or in dreams.
The words of his will were blades
 for ripping apart—
  fraying forever the knots of kinship—
  even in my dreams.

SANS SELVAGE 2

Some dreams close with a selvage finish…
but not the ones that have me searching,
walking alone and fearfully on Howard Avenue at night,
an old brick street that I know,
yet one that does not lead home.
Then I know there is no home:
it is as gone as childhood,
gone with the lives once shared by mine.

Familial circle rent,
pulled loose by roots of time.
Outsider I will always be,
bereft of home-bound roads,
bound to a homeless destiny—
wandering an endless maze.

OWL OF WARNING

It was a surprise to hear
 a haunting screech of warning
 lashing out from the elm tree,
 coming from a little owl
 in the darkening twilight.
He watched me steadily as I
 brooded on his mythology: Harbinger of Death.
Too late to warn me, Owl.
My brother-in-law died yesterday.
We would all have wished
 his going without the ventilator
 these last two weeks,
 before the mind had died.

LUCY BATTLE

Lucy wove her spell
  from the heart of the yellow brick house
  full of well-chosen books, furnishings, mementoes
  among soft-spoken pines on the lake
  smiling veranda overlook
  that hosted spirit breeze filled with birdsong.

Her spell was a tapestry of love--
  Lucy and Jean—handholders, partners
  Lucy and Carol
  Lucy and Robert
  Lucy and Greg
  Lucy and Suzanna:
Tapestry of loving heartholders
  stitchery that touched her students and friends
  and stretched to Alabama family.

Her soulful listening was done with
sparkling eye, graceful wit—
her long-remembered monogram.

Maria Courtens Janner: January 11, 1925- May 13, 2008
from war to peace as
soldier
educator
wife
mother
homemaker
artist
actress

Maria kept her friendships long
much like her long red hair
not shortened all life long.
Her own and others' children—and ourselves—
 caught her generous gamin-spirit,
her elfin caprices, inquiries, explorations,
enthusiasms that stretched the mind and
showed the artist's eye, the actor's gift.
We revere her personal bravery
in her Holland homeland,
overrun by tyrants,
as she rode her bicycle into the countryside
with messages for the underground network.
We can't forget what Maria left:
for Suzette, for Joyce and Fred, for Georgette and Alex,
for Freddy and Johnny and Alexis
and for all of us—
so much life and love to savor,
to embellish our lives and history forever.

LEAVING HOME

Loquats lullaby the cradled windows
big oaks sway across the roof;
　their murmurs echo all the secrets
　leavings, returnings, lovings, missings.

Father's paintings taken down
Mother's glassware, china homeless now
　mahogany buffet gone to a new home.

How do you say goodbye to a home?
　With a sigh, with a tear in the eye,
　with festered feelings
　in corners of the heart
　in closets of memory
　with deep sighs and tears in the eyes.

Still squirrels come looking lakeside;
　mallards with maverick white gander
　come searching too for handouts.
They don't hear the sighs
　or see the tears in the eyes.
They seek the new hands scattering handouts.

IT BEGAN WITH A BROKEN DOLL

It began with a broken doll:
smithereens of a smashed porcelain head
on the sidewalk,
my childish sobs foretelling
later life-losses, who knew when.

Already motherless,
I knew my fosterhood
which changed three times.

Break away—on my own—
no prodding, leaving home and family,
always trying to
make and gather my own family.

Going West, going North, going South
and making my own family.

HELEN SAFARA

February 16, 1920-July 16, 2008

There is a Helen place, a spiritual web
 that caught us, each one
 and held us closely for the gifts she gave—
years of giving to family and friends
 from Wisconsin to Florida and especially to Doe Ridge.
There were rhubarb pie, barbecued chicken, biscuits and more.
Helen was an organizer: our door-to-door mail service
 on Doe Ridge was Helen's gift.
Our Neighborhood Watch was one of her projects.
With a deep laugh and a good joke
 Helen could stride across life's prickly pathways.
And her compassionate commitment to justice
 could reflect on the bare spots of our neglect.
Spirit Helen tells us love, courage, generosity.

FAREWELL TO MISS B

What is that floppy, smudgy, lifeless-looking
 thing in Astrid's arms?

It's Miss B cuddled up against her chest,
 that cloth dog, at least nine years old,
 the one who has heard many private words
 and kept her secrets well,
 the one requiring a trip back
 to a restaurant where she was left,
 the one who has traveled by plane and by car,
 the one who's gone to many sleepovers
 where each sleepover-guest dangled and cuddled
 her own Miss B in between
 some rock and roll dancing.

Miss B's days are numbered now.
She's about to make an exit.
Astrid is wearing a training bra.

FOR MARY AND MARTIN

How they cling to one another—
my college friend and her husband—
after the uneven seasons of sixty years
(best years, yesteryears, lost years).
Now their only daughter's sudden death
shrouds the conversation,
etches once again deep loss lines
on the gravestone of memory,
recalls the loss of their only son
when in his twenties.
The banter today is a gentle plucking of heartstrings,
an interlude in their strict Judaic mourning,
a summation of six lives:
two parents, two lost children,
two adopted grandsons without a mother.
Caring words assuage some anguish,
wrap the memories, tie them up
as presents tagged for sharing.

THAT'S MOLLY

Molly my meow mistress
 orders me "right NOW"
 or "all RIGHT"
 after fixing her stare on me
 to be certain I heard
 what her deafness defeats.
Her watching posts
 are hallways and doors—
 no escape--"oh YEAHWR"—
 her timing impeccable
 for mealtimes,
 possible water games
 with a cup in the shower
 for her to knock over and toss about,
 and outdoor trips to drink
 from the air conditioner's drip.
"RROWR, MORRR, RRP, RRP"…

WOOKIE, OUR LOVING CAT

Wookie was a loving cat
who sought your lap
for a loving pat
and purred resounding thanks.
His eloquent meows
bespoke his heritage
which must have been
of some part Siamese.
We admired his long legs and dainty feet,
with poised toes that pointed outward.
Our dark grey feline
was our friend for 21 years.

GRIZZ RULED TILL 2008

His aggravating ways still
 have me conditioned to put
  the food beyond his reach.
How many times he ate
 my lunch or breakfast or supper!
I won't have to warn my dinner guests:
 Delay for half an hour.
 Grizz just ate the whole corned beef!

I miss his fiercely-barked announcements:
 The mailman is here.
 The UPS man is here.
 Some stranger is at the door.

Each morning he sized up my shoes.
He knew which ones were meant for a walk.
Say the word "treat" for lightning response
 unless a possum was in the yard.
On a breezy day his nose lifted
 toward all the scents a dog should know.

My neighbor's cat is camped out
 in the driveway and knows—Grizz is gone.
I miss his nightly in-house prowl
 to check on all of us.
I miss that much-loved dog of elkhound mix.

SYMPHONIES

Borodin's symphony is digging a grave
in the bottomless part of my heart
a booming prelude
wrenching out my secrets
arranged in bearable hiding.
The notes of loud staccato
lay bare what no one can know.

All my hurt is hushed
when the pizzicato of Tschaikowsky
plays remembered happiness—
a college lounge in view
discoveries made new
mastery, mystery awaiting.

BICYCLE RIDER

His sleeveless shirt balloons
 from the breeze he makes
 while pedaling rapidly beside my Jetta.

His longish hair is clinging sweatily
 and I imagine how pungent are his armpits
 on this overheated August day.
I once had said that pungency evoked
  the hairy armpits of a workman
 exuding strength of arms and torso.

I am 86, he's maybe 36
 but a pheromonal fantasy arises
 with the passage of this rider.
I haven't forgotten.

MY BROKEN TOE

I will rise above my broken toe,
I refuse to let it slow
my goings to or fro.
This crooked digit
makes me fidget
makes me want to show
how fast, how fleet my feet CAN go!

MENU FOR BAD DREAMS

Pureed black bean soup, so savory;
 sharp and hot green peppers
 and rich sardines in oil.
 No wonder my midnight snack
 brought black dreams and green grotesqueries
 and painful tidal waves to my innards—
  with few regrets!

CHIHULY GLASS

Sea-forms, free-forms
prismatic glass-scapes
ceiling-floor mille fleurs reiterated
vitreous dialogues with light
refractions of refractions incandescing
through fire-born blue, red, vermillion, purple, pearl,
gold, green gardens of perfumed glass
lollipop sheen for the eye to devour.

BLUE JAY

Hey, blue jay! Why do you fuss at me ?
I fill your feeder, I pay the taxes,
you live here rent-free.
Yes, your blue and black outfit
is haughty and snappy.
 I would rather hear
your come-hither call with the trill,
your invitation to watch you strut.

CHIRPER

Little two-note chirper
yellow breast-feathers
and a fuzzy head
never seen here before
now calls all day
for the past week.
He never leaves my yard.
Is he lost or a new habitué?

BAIT

He was ugly and menacing
with his crusty mandibles awaiting prey,
black triangled legs
striking a position to spring.
But who got the fatal bite?
June bug or his nemesis?

GOLD WING VISIT

Sparkle yellow butterfly
 two-winged glint of gold
 that tips the sticky pollen
 on an open red hibiscus--
 a quick caress of petal lips
 and then the winged sunbeam
 glows on flame-red rose.
From there to burnished Canna lily
 flashing sunset-sunrise chroma
 filtered through a green leaf screen.
My day now glistens gold although
 this flickering, fluttering butterfly
 soon mounts the breeze and blue sky
 for some other gardens where
 gleaming wings will gild again with pollen-paint.

IF I COULD TALK BIRDTALK

If I could talk birdtalk I would ask them:
  Why do you shun the caterpillars on my oleander?
I entreat you, bluejays, wrens, woodpeckers, mockingbirds,
  to savor something live and juicy,
  with colorful black hairy spikes on orange seersucker body.

And look!My feathered frolickers,
  why do you ignore the cadres of invading beetles,
  black and red, benign but pestiferous,
  swarming, copulating incessantly,
  covering the walls of my house,
  sneaking through doors,
  embarrassing me in front of company?
Perhaps they know I don't use spray
  so I swat hordes of them at a time.
I pick off the camouflaged caterpillars, avenge myself by stomping the beetles.

NO MATE MI CULEBRA!

Is he/she one among others?
Finally warmer weather brought
a black snake,
slender three feet of slither
whose folds unfolded speedily
across the patio
into a forest of plumbago.
The sleek culebra was sighted again
coiled against a wall
near the garbage can
extending a vertical probe
with his flickering tongue.
My maid raised her mop
and fearfully said,"Mata?"
I said, "No mate, es buena culebra!"
However, I look carefully when I weed
and I might jump if it
surprises me when parked at a flower pot.

PROMISE

Another full moon
 sneaks through my window,
 at perigee appearing
 with insinuated promise,
 a promise pressed to breast
 awaiting arms of affirmation.

SUBURBAN EGRET

Startling to see him standing
motionless in the median of the parking lot
a curving contrast against the grass and asphalt
all alert for lizards
long legs poised for pounce and snatch
long neck arching for the catch
white-feathered emblem of encroachment—his and ours.

THE CHIRPER AGAIN

The one-note chirper has returned
 to lament I know not what.
 Is it a sad song of summer's farewell?
 Or is it welcome to fall's flags
 of changing colors?
Bees so busy on my yellowing raintrees;
 days drifting sooner into night;
 and more moonlight-silvered hours.

THE GARDEN SECTION

Down the aisle of Lowe's garden section
  amidst purple petunias and pansies
  and golden marigolds—
  all awaiting spring planting—
  a wayward bee is buzzing a pink begonia.

Did he hitchhike here by truck
  or wing it dead-reckoning by scent or breeze?

Spring is artificial here
  but the flowers are real.

WELCOME TO MY PERIWINKLES

Stark against a stony wall
 where I had counted not at all
 to have a periwinkle, rooted feet
 pushed down between concrete,
 there my uninvited plants luxuriate,
 uncultivated blooms proliferate.
There was hardly room
 for flowers to bloom
 in that corner of utility
 where trash cans, rank hostility,
 I thought, defied fertility.
Persistent periwinkles, born to endure
 the slights of man, to inure
 themselves to sand and concrete,
 drought and careless feet.
Welcome to my periwinkles, looking sprightly,
 giving grace to a site unsightly.

AFTER CHRISTMAS

Santa Clause is folded, put in a drawer.
The cardboard H A P P Y H O L I D A Y S
is collapsed like the old year,
hidden away.

We felt the passage, whisked away
like brown leaves, trodden amorphous heaps,
reminders of our celebrated moments,
moments that return again in season.

HOLLY TREE ON PICWOOD ROAD

A second look showed me red berries
(I have passed that tree innumerable times on a dogwalk)
but I barely saw them among the holly's leaves
a waxy wreath for winter's holiday;

tendered for our solstice
as much as mistletoe.

HYMNING SUNDAY

Sweet tranquility
 neighborhood at rest
  morning shadows a bit longer
  dog out for a stroll
  sniffing, marking,
  alert as an elkhound can be
  but missing the mailman's alarming approach;
   one frantic husband
   clawing at the curbside water cutoff
   wife bent over—with advice?
Sleepers late abed, catching up
 not yet the lawnmowers, hedgeclippers.
Some neighbors off to church—not I
My altar rises radiant
 sunlit green, leafy holiness in raintree spires.
Believers, come sit in my swing
 and sing with me the flower-song.

SEASONAL SUITE

Christmas
Driveways stacked with Christmas debris
holiday wrappings declaring the end
big toy boxes emptied of their surprises.
Garbage trucks trolling the streets,
the season settles down serenely
to await the next ecclesiastical event
or pagan celebration
or rites of spring, summer, fall.

Summer Spell
Cicadas' chorus broadcasting
temperature readings, taken from tree to tree,
twilight brings a spell.
I am spellbound
by cicada choristers.
I hum with their twilight drumming.

Rain Lilies
Faint blue rain lilies
starred overnight all over my lawn
to let me know how welcome is the rain.
The mower will cut them down,
but leave their radiance in pink-tinged blue.

TO GEORGIA O'KEEFE

It could be Georgia's magnolia
 blooming on this tall magnolia tree
 a reproduction of her giantism
 traced from canvas to branch.

But I know it's not her white-petaled giant
 lavish among more modest tree-blooms,
 for many reasons:

Could she color a whiff of magnolia's
 springtime giddiness?
Did she ever mark the browning
 of these stately flowers?
Or paint the eruption of furry cones ?
Or sketch the curled-up leaves
 that nag our noisy footsteps?

WINTER-HAIKU

Winter warmth is too unseasonal.
A freeze will come
to blight the buds.

WARM AND WRAINY

Soft, soft summer rain
 veils our neighborhood—
 nothing new here—
 a block away the sun is bearing down.

Days and days of this monsoon
 stewing all things right
 for mushrooms overnight
 to sprout in clustered cozy collusion
 with the vital drizzle.

Runaway vines gallop a foot a day.

TROPICAL AUGUST

You don't deceive me, nut grass,
 when your runners easily pass
 along three feet below ground
 then choose to erupt above ground
 mimicking the lawn grass.
How coy your slender blades can be!
You sprout again where I pulled you free
 just yesterday before the rain
 that called you forth again.
My tortured fingers cramp with pain.

SPRING BREAKOUT

Balky spring at last
 brought my amaryllis to glory
 with a show of scarlet.
Raindrops in the night
 washed away the hesitation,
 opened another flaming bud,
 perked up the bougainvillea
 where a daring mockingbird
 nested amid thorns and purple petals.
What a scold that bird is.
When the kitchen door is opened
 he flaunts his ownership
 and chirps me back to my domain.

ON STAGE

Blue cobalt petals answer the curtain call
 when sun-up cues the matinee.
By afternoon they bow out
 with a green petal-closure.
So does the creeping buttercup
 when summoned by the sun
 to stage its brief part in the show.
Nighttime brings a jasmine gala,
 pungent pheremones flung for
little white moths
 that pirouette among
 the yellow and fuschia throats.
And once in a while
 a big proboscis moth stops by.

MY WOEFUL CANDELARIAS

It was the frost god that blistered us
 with biting, blighting, baleful breath of January,
 that harshly singed my selloums, vincas and poinsettias,
 that flambéed my candelarias before blooming
 and torched the tiny orange trumpet-clusters
 into a sagging bedraggle.
I will not forgive that demon
 for sparing my perpetual invader.
Why couldn't he have slain that
 sneaky, serpentine vine coiled everywhere,
 no matter how many times it is pulled,
 and always sneering greenwise at me?

MOCKINGBIRD VESPERS

I thought he was singing to me—
those vesperal trills, too-whees and tch-tch-tches.
But he flew his evensong away
no doubt to a feathered friend.
The silence lasted until cicadas churred
crescendo-decrescendo with darkening rhythm.
My forced retreat gave way
to gnats and a buzz of mosquitoes.

MONSOON

So welcome was the rain
that I opened the door
to see the curtain outside,
cascades from the eaves,
plumbago gulping all it could.
Thousands of thirsts were quenched
that evening for the
green matinee next day.

LE BALLET DU GARBAGE
(IN CARROLLWOOD)

Driving behind the garbage truck
I witnessed a weird ballet—
a pas de deux between man and machine.
The dancer's pas de chat were lithe with
retrievals of barrels, sometimes
tossed and emptied with one hand.
His arabesques propelled him
back to a ledge on the metallic maw
where rapid footsteps
and arcking legs
prepared the next great leap.
The dancing slowed me, moved me
along the practice path of one balletomane.

JULY SWELTERS

These swift showers storm in circles
catching us along our busy dailiness
sweeping away the morning sun
too fast for us to get to shelter
without umbrellas' partial protection.

Rumbling on across our rampant yards
the rain leaves roads that smoke
grass grown taller
vines that overnight have closed the gate
small toads not seen for years
rain lilies starring pale amethyst
and then July's hot-as-hell sun in the afternoon.

Let's make mint juleps!

IT'S SOUTHERN

Mocking birds and magnolias
 twang my inner Southern today
 where heart-home glows
 where jasmine claims its rites
 where the whip-poor-will sings night songs
 where woodpecker nesters trill continuo.
Soft days and evenings until
 stormy summer takes our breath away.
My dog will languish in the house,
 lose his lust for the scent of snakes,
 forget the fuss he raised at squirrels.
We both regard the sun, look for shade
 and seek clouds and canopies of trees.

IF WINTER COMES

It's January but my rain trees
 are only half bereft of leaves
 that should have left by September.

Laggard leaves and seed-pods
 drag out their messy demise.

They wait for a storm that stalls
 at the edge of winter.

Their remaining greenery
 is half-hearted in this pause of seasons.

HEAT ALERT

June has stumbled, forgotten
 how we need the rain—
 no pelting pacifiers
 for our gardens or my overheated self.
Gasping heat alerts
 bear down to melt ambitions
 assail our good intentions
 for our chores outdoors.
The heat has hushed the neighborhood.
Our only music is
 the orchestra of air conditioners.

DAY/NIGHT VERSE

I would like
to poetize each day,
lengthen its leaving,
wrap its aura
like a shawl against the night.

A SEASONING

Fall blew us a Florida seasoning,
  sharpened the gibbous moon,
  served it crisply, waferly, platter-wise
  for our appraising moonlit eyes.

A dash of brown seed-pods on the rain tree
  left their limbs in a hurry
  and heaped together with fallen yellow flowers.
Velvet matting underfoot, fusion of cool and colors.

Why so late this year?
We wonder why September's exit collided with October.

BEFORE THE RAINS COME

My yard apologizes
 for its withered grass,
 this unbecoming in-between.

How limp plumbago looks,
 like blue-flowered skirts
 that lost their starch.

MARCH 2007

After the shower the sky was piercing blue
  pierced itself by
  cloudships billowed on their way to spring.
The sun laid a welcome mat of shadows
  beneath the rinsed-out trees.
Rivets of this ritual burned warm within me
  melted sadness
  sent me skyward
  joining a half-circle of ibises
  already turned to vernal March.

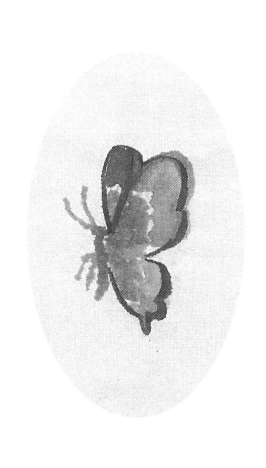

FILINGS

Emery-board news rubs my feelings raw
when reading:"27 Afghan civilians killed."
So sorry, says our military when totaling
the costs of "democratizing" and de-stabilizing
clans or Kabul or other places.
Our rubble and rot expose
our leavings in Iraq
where slaughter still goes on.

EYE-SIGHT

Eyes meet other eyes
 brimming with colors:
 all the shared songs are lingering there,
 all the past words are writ within.

A wink is as good as a smile.

Seen close your bluest blue allures,
 gives an aura-certitude
 to the net we share,
 to the filaments of what we know.

Our eyes will limn the infinite circle.

EXCHANGE

A dose of Pepto-/Bismol
  will settle my dismal
  digestive tract in pain
  but won't relieve the strain
  of sipping chicken soup
  too constantly to suit
  my taste for all things spicy—
  which now and then is dicey.
I need to find a wizard
  to trade my gullet for a gizzard.

I HEARD A DOG BARK

I heard a dog bark in the night
and it reminded me of
all the lonely nights of youth and age.

Why does such loneliness insinuate
 itself with that dog's unanswered bark?

Dark of night, dark of heart—
and a dog's barking tells me
loneliness is worse with age.

As lonely too as the whistle of a train—
a freight train that waddled at night
within our hearing
on its way to Port Tampa.

Trains of thoughts now switched to sidings
as lonely as that whistle or that bark.

LIFETIMES

Then is now
a glint of now and then
a film run forward and backward
sound unwound with leit-motif
of childish cries or patter
a how it was and when
descant of lovers' lingerings
refrains to stretch a lifetime
blazoned travels in a shimmer
dream or reel—
our codes are real and now.
Our calendars dance a sarabande
with then and now.

NEW ORLEANS: IN MEMORIAM

It's not the city I saw in World War II--
  French Quarter bars, bistros, cafes
  French coffee brewing strong
  dubonnet cocktails, Pat O'Brien's,
  stingers, Antoine's,
  absinthe frappes, The Absinthe House,
  brandy, shrimp remoulade.

Walking Jackson Square with Jean Lafitte's ghost,
four of us together wrote a poem
in a sazerac fever
and sense turned to nonsense with daylight.

Now it's a wounded animal
bleeding sewage, filth, spilled oil, human detritus.
Jazz blues sing in tones of dark gray,
an ending note keyed to hope.

ON THE STREET CORNERS

Wraiths at so many street corners
with supplicating signs—
food, money, work—
I dare not look.
Once there was a pregnant woman!
Where is home?
Is it a cardboard box?
Is it made of blankets or plastic?
We know the address:
nowhere in this town.

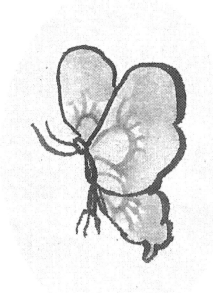

ON FRANZ KAFKA'S "METAMORPHOSIS"

I cried over Kafka's cockroach
metamorphosed into a husk
by the daily grind of labor Chaplinesque,
to think a wayward foot
could crunch, obliterate,
even a mother's or father's foot,
might leave behind the grieving parents
of this cucaracha.

What did I fear?

Cucarachismo is what I feared
from our societal coils
that tangle foot and mind--
and I feared for my offspring, setting off
for an unseen metamorphic mainland,
though I hoped they could side-step
those strangulating coils.

POWER-FULL

Beneath the vertical power pole
he stands hip-deep in the hole
he digs by hand
and his hand-power
drenches his black skin.

It's above 90 degrees today.

Power in the wires above
unseen power to
move all our machines
to broadcast way too much palaver.

But today we need
that powerful
working-man's hand and shovel.

ROSETTA STONE

I am looking for a Rosetta Stone
 among my craggy decades piled high
 with zigs and zags worked into them.

Perhaps a cave within the crags
 is hiding more than one stone,
 crystal clues still undiscovered.

Such thought seems reasonable,
 lures me into searching further,
 seeking translations immutable.

There might be storied omens among
 the gravel of the nearby past,
 blurry in a burnt sienna desert.

SPRING FALLOUT

1960's Sometime

Purple tears lie on azalea blooms,
 the dogwood weeps a white lament.
The dew's a dirge, a scourge on all the earth.
Spring rains a plague, irradiated contempt.
The meadow mourns its roots of evil
 cursed with poisonous grass blades
 thrust at mankind's jugular.
Mushroom clouds bear deadly spores for earth-spawn,
 exacting rites of non-fertility—
 stillborn genes and chromosomes
 offered up to lunacy.

STARING DOWN THE BASILISK

I will stare down that mythical monster—
the basilisk of elderhood.
With his ossifying glance
he comes at me sideways,
tries to nick my composure
unsettle my wits and
mess with my digits.

But he belongs not here but there
in the ancient books
or a moldy trunk
filled with withered papers
stamped with falsehoods.

I will bury that chimera
with his awful gaze
beneath the crushing cairn of time.

TECO'S TOWERS
(TAMPA ELECTRIC COMPANY)

(Linebaugh Avenue through Egypt Lake Neighborhood)
2007

They marched by stealth
 through the neighborhood
  up and down the front and back streets.

Juggernauts led the electric charge
 with giant spindles of cable
  strung so deliberately
  so ugly with their insulators—
  ugliness that spun away
  from central ganglia.

Electrified assault upon the people!
Towers of TECO
 bearing transformers
 humming with derision
 pointing skyward
 dwarfing trees and homes
 in a transfigured neighborhood.

THE DEFIANCE OF ABRAHAM

Abraham's arm was raised
 for the killing blow to his son—
 God's demand.
But another voice
 intoned an otherwise.
Defiance saved the son.
Paternity was sanctified.
Now our sons follow
 orders to death.
Where are the arms that
 would refuse to strike ?
Whose inner-voiced defiance
 will save our sons
 from "righteous battles" ?

THE TAKEOVER

Thin white skin of shoreline
 stretches from delta to marshes
 to bays and bayous and beyond,
 bejeweled strand along the Gulf
 faceted with fins and wings
 and other things along the beach.
All are sinking in a mire
 of integumentary insult
 inflamed with black and orange ooze.
Beached black tarball eyes wash up
  from a spewing monster below
  to tell with deadening eyes
 what befell below from arrogance and avarice.

WRAPPED IN PLASTIC

Bicycle rider burdened with bags
 hanging in front, hanging on sides,
 bags of burdens, parts of his life?
His heaviness weighs on me,
 the burdens are mine—
 our lives touch quickly
 in my turn lane and his turn lane—
 a moment's regard
 a turn of thought
and what is bagged in plastic passes on.

TROGLODYTES

Vernal Equinox 2005

Miners they are:
But it's the news they delve into with shafts of disconnect;
vocal picks parting the words and action from all veins of human ore.

We are Platonic troglodytes trapped in a cavern, straining to see light,
watching the stealth of stalagmites—happenings posited by broadcasters,
events gouached in meaningless chiaroscuro.
Hacksters, hucksters, mucksters—abroad—
Pity us.

DOE RIDGE

Boone, NC

This old house built 45 years ago by a mountain man
has windowed eyes atop the ridge
looking over a narrow valley, a cauldron
where thick fog boils up after summer showers.

We are now and then visitors
who share the summit
with birds, deer, turkeys and chipmunks.

Long gone are the builder Ron and winter overseer Venie
both tobacco chewers.

Venie who canned, crafted quilts and milked her cow
and went into mourning when she had to give up the cow,
who called her sister across the road to listen with her phone to
Venie's radio playing gospel music.
She listened to the police radio all the time.
Did those reports confirm her fear
of imminent judgment from the Lord?
She said the earthquake one year was certainly a sign.
She never believed we put an astronaut on the moon.

Ron was stone and brick mason, electrician, carpenter,
finish man and wood artisan
but he built his house right next to Howard's Creek
which took part of his house in an angry torrent one year.
Ron lost two wives to cancer.

STORM ON DOE RIDGE

The mountains purpled with a coming storm.
Thunder wracked the ridges.
All the creatures stilled themselves
as apoplectic winds and lightning lashed the peaks.
Hollows quivered with the onslaught,
creeks and branches shrilled with strain.
Afterward the valleys sighed a thankful mist.

WALK ON DOE RIDGE

It was not a gallop going up,
 but quicker, surer footsteps
 some years ago made the ridge
 slope with easier access.
Today the climb was slower
 and measured by more years.

July's array was all along the road:
 daylilies in yellow cascades,
 bee-balm spiked with lavender and gray,
 burdock topped with purple starbursts
 awaiting autumn's snagging stickers,
 blackberry brambles loaded with green berries,
 shy ferns hiding in the shade,
 along with bright red turk's cap
 not sure if sun or shade is better.

A year has punished once-regal hemlocks
 with the wooly adelgid worm
 whose appetite has skeletonized the trees.
And after forty years the does and fawns
 are back to claim and name their ridge.

GHOSTS ON DOE RIDGE

Fireflies in the meadow brush my dreams
 of those departed: two friends, a husband, a lover—
 not to mention scattered children and grandchildren.

On my porch at night the trees sing of times remembered—
 names whispered with the raspy leaves.

In shadowed darkness a twig will snap
 and break the quiet as
 a walker in the woods seeks us unsought.
Stepping-stones have a ghostly imprint of who put them there.
My two dogs have come and gone but
 their marks will linger on the trails.

How many full moons lit the way for goings and comings,
 up the ridge, down the ridge
 to Howard's Creek and beyond
 where the big falls and the lesser falls
 echo among the boulders.

All of you may come again for you were always welcome.

POSSESSION (HURRICANE 2004)

My house is mine again
  after the fearful winds
  tried my spirits,
tried the tree spirits,too,
with furious fists hurling ghostly
blows against my windows,
making oak trees rain down snares
of leaves and sticks.

Inside my house the darkness
blotted out familiar shapes.
Imagined demons pounded on my portals,
howled among deep shadows,
mocked my candlelight.

Next day: the sun, cleanup, neighbors sweeping and raking,
lifting of the beaten flower-heads confirming my ownership—
until the next storm comes.

DRAGOON MOUNTAINS

Composed in Tombstone, Arizona 1940

Sentinels of the desert stand
staunchly guarding their no-man's land
while sinking sun transforms each spire
with magic phosphorescent fire
and silhouettes the trees
that firmly hold to stony knees.

The deep blue shadows emphasize
where gaping crevice lies.
Above the glowing, rugged peaks
setting sun lastly seeks
where glorious clouds are rolled
to burnish them with gold.

On high majestic mountain chain
and lesser hills across the plain
the dragoon soldiers stand sedate
as if deciding each one's fate.

MOON PHASES

I In a blue rice paper sky an early moon is etched
   full and flanked by starry clouds outstretched.

II Twilight moon, round and liquefied by sunglow pink,
   hung back until
   the June-brief night
   hung unstarred backdrop
   for its unmatched moonstone
   fastened briefly at the darkening sky-throat of night.

COMET EXPLOSION

Cometized by NASA,
    pointed at a galaxy to peer at an eyeless mote
    peerless precision, bending back time
    aeons in our hands to show what could be done on Earth.
Instead we precisely atomize our bloodkin, our cities, our land.

DIALOGUES

I hear a caw-cus of crows in my treetop
and I am sure they know what they are talking about.

Their crow-conversation must cover
wind and rain, waterholes and seed sources,
the chief crow and he- and she- crows
and the two hawks circling above.

Crow specifics. Species certainty.
Crow cussing and discussing, crow percussion.
Woe to the wayward.

Is it true of our species?
The ones with black halos, black knobs in ears
and umbilicals feeding on blather in the ether.
Words and music bang about cyberially
but beg the bigger questions.
What are the questions or the answers?
So many unseen, unanswered speakers.

ONCE THERE WAS A MILKY WAY

From the starscape
 ancient eyes imprinted sea-paths and Earth-paths.
Cairns and monoliths bespoke
  celestial messages from
  Milky Way's millions of luminaries—
 translations into stone-marked circles and graveled medicine-wheels.
Sky-time.
Distant stars bright enough to tell star-time and moon-time
 before the sun arose.

How bright the stars were
 before we lit our nightscape
 and blotted out so many star-eyes,
 before we yielded to the rapture of neon.

We are alit so wholly that
 shadows flee from urbanscape,
 allowing only blazoned sun, moon or glimmer of stars.

REVELATIONS OF THE HUBBLE TELESCOPE

When I see the Hubble photographs
  my small world shrivels smaller
  at the near end of the telescope.

What narrative is written in this universe
  in these redshift reckonings?

I see a crucible for stars,
  a galactic glimpse of creations
  where Earth is peering at some imagined purpose
  across millions of light years—
  lens pointed at billions of stars and suns
  where nebular clouds explode
  into anthropomorphic forms.

But this end of the overseeing monster
  is where the fires begin,
  the lights illuminate,
  my spirit catches fire,
  where Earth is balancing its gases,
  fending off cosmic rays,
  nurturing all of life
  with oceans, mountains, land and infinite DNA.

GLOBAL CONVERSATION

Man:Abstract
Words:Abstract
Spirals wound unnumbered times—
non-Pierian springs
bounced backward to themselves—
never arcking—
  lost transcontinentally
    among the final filaments
    of multivalent universes
coiled and fused-frozen
cable, satellite, tube

LUNAR ROVER RAMBLING ON THE MOON

Giant-stepper on our moon-mate,
 brainchild of our earthmen,
 bouncing about Orion's measured moonscape
 describing the circular,elliptical
 rigidity of earthbound minds
 cast in moonrock to mock
 our stunted children—
 those who need a giant step along
 the light-year path to life.

COMPUTER CREEP

Is it friend or foe?
It spooks me when I need it,
DELETE can emasculate a manuscript.
It tingles my trembling fingers.
Between pc and printer—disconnect!
Reconnect during the night unnoticed!!
Journey resumed on its own path. Not mine.
Delicately finger-tipping
 I corral the creep.

CYBERIA

Orbits studded with satellites
 circling techno-bits
 overwhelming our systems.

Winken, Blinken and Nod never knew
or fished for such stellar orbiters.

We harvest our celestial ocean.
We find our geopositions.
We gather swarms of soundbites
 netted for our Earthlings.

FLETCHER AND 22ND STREET

I in my Subaru glide smoothly through
  a street lined with misery.
At Fletcher and 22nd Street
  my glance tries to avoid the scene
  but guilt plucks out the unavoidable,
  the on-foot shoppers, the WalMarters, daring all drivers;
  the man with a cane hobbling lamely across the Stygian asphalt;
  the man driving a scooter in the street;
  and a young man on crutches.

"Suitcase City" spills its contents,
  coming or going they pass
  the VA Hospital, the University, too.

Almost hidden near garbage cans
  the remnants of a once-family panhandles a meager crowd.

The sun shines on us all.
  It makes a day and then more days.

AT THE EDGE OF MY NEIGHBORHOOD

At the edge of my neighborhood
 the road curves away
 but an empty plastic jug
 in a corner of the playground
 forces me to look.

For a moment this wanton waste
 accelerates my haste
 to leave somebody's debris,
 leftover insult—rudeness on the grass.

Its mark is on my mind.

SILVER AND BLACK

Moonlight smudges and softens
 as the sun descends
 from silvered light and inky shadows,
 moves away from remaining silhouettes.
The arch of sky is bending light-to-dark
 leaving the moonlight moving
 toward its setting
 rearranging our dreams.